TO:

_____

FROM:

_____

DATE:

_____

Copyright © 2018 by B&H Publishing Group
Printed in China
978-1-5359-1474-1

All Scripture quotations are taken from the Christian Standard Bible®,
Copyright © 2017 by Holman Bible Publishers. Used by permission.
Christian Standard Bible® and CSB® are federally registered
trademarks of Holman Bible Publishers.

1 2 3 4 5 6 7 8 • 22 21 20 19 18

*Do not fear, for I am with you;
do not be afraid, for I am your God.
I will strengthen you; I will help you;
I will hold on to you with my righteous right hand.
~Isaiah 41:10~*

www.mooschead lake.com

Greenville = chalet mooschead
207-695-2950

moosehead

Greenville Realty (century 21)
207-695-3731
Debbie (207-717-4905)
4950)

Septic =
well =

Joe
~~270~~ - 280 - 3300
207

> *Be strong and courageous; don't be terrified or afraid of them. For the LORD your God is the one who will go with you; he will not leave your or abandon you.*
> *–Deuteronomy 31:6–*

> Therefore we do not give up. Even though our outer person is being destroyed, our inner person is being renewed day by day.
> -2 Corinthians 4:16–18-

> *Trust in the LORD with all your heart, and do not rely on your own understanding.*
> *~Proverbs 3:5~*

> *Because of the Lord's faithful love we do not perish, for his mercies never end. They are new every morning; great is your faithfulness!*
> *—Lamentations 3:22–23—*

> Do nothing out of selfish ambition or conceit, but in humility consider others as more important than yourselves.
> -Philippians 2:3-

Let us run with endurance the race that lies before us, keeping our eyes on Jesus, the source and perfecter of our faith.
-Hebrews 12:1–2-

> *The one who walks with the wise will become wise, but a companion of fools will suffer harm.*
> *-Proverbs 13:20-*

> I have been crucified with
> Christ, and I no longer live,
> but Christ lives in me.
> ~Galatians 2:20~

*Trust in the L*ORD *forever,
because in the L*ORD*, the L*ORD
himself, is an everlasting rock!
~Isaiah 26:4~

The Lord does not delay his promise, as some understand delay, but is patient with you, not wanting any to perish but all to come to repentance.
-2 Peter 3:9-

> Blessed is the one who endures trials, because when he has stood the test he will receive the crown of life that God has promised to those who love him.
> -James 1:12-

*But I know that
my Redeemer lives, and at
the end he will stand on the dust.*
-Job 19:25-

> *Rejoice always, pray constantly,
> give thanks in everything;
> for this is God's will for you
> in Christ Jesus.*
> *~1 Thessalonians 5:16–18~*

> "Haven't I commanded you
> you: be strong and courageous?
> Do not be afraid or dicouraged,
> for the LORD your God is with
> you wherever you go."
> -Joshua 1:9-

> "The LORD your God is among you, a warrior who saves. He will rejoice over you with gladness. He will be quiet in his love. He will delight in you with singing."
> ~Zephaniah 3:17~

> "Come to me, all of you who are weary and burdened, and I will give you rest."
> -Matthew 11:28-

> And be kind and compassionate
> to one another, forgiving
> one another, just as God also
> forgave you in Christ.
> ~Ephesians 4:32~